My Quiet Place
Adult Coloring Book Vol. 1

25 Relaxing Kaleidoscope-Style Coloring Designs

by Michael Santini

www.facebook.com/adultcoloringbookscentral

Introduction

There are times in our busy lives when we all need to find our "quiet place". Taking some time alone to relax, clear our minds and recharge is important for our health and well being.

Coloring is a great way to find and enjoy your quiet place – and the 25 designs in this adult coloring book were created to help you do just that.

Inside this book you will find a range of patterns – from easy to challenging. Choose the one that calls out to you and start coloring.

All the designs are printed on one side, so you can use your favorite medium – colored pencils, pens or crayons – to color with.

I hope you enjoy turning the designs in this book into your own personal works of art!

- Michael Santini

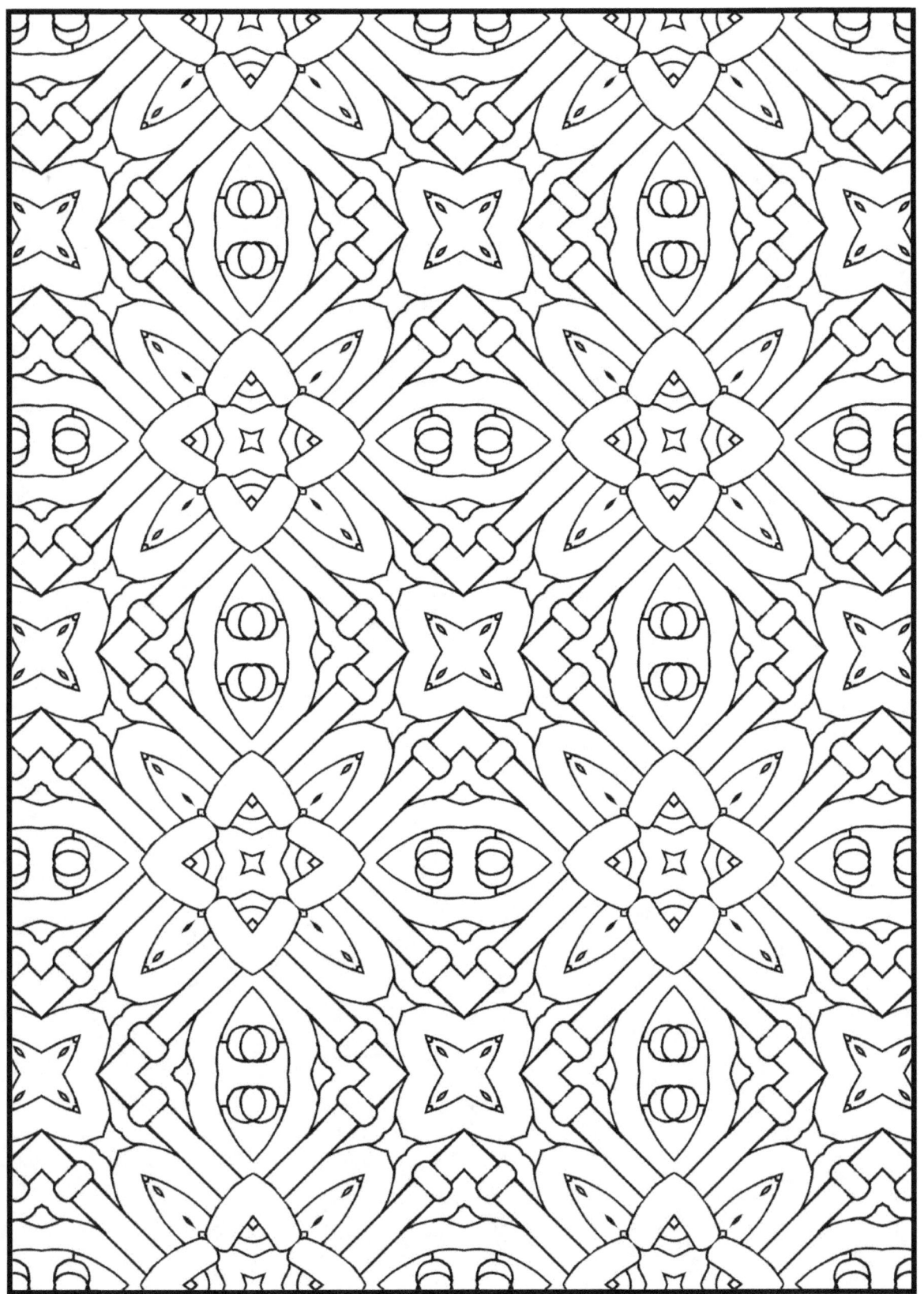

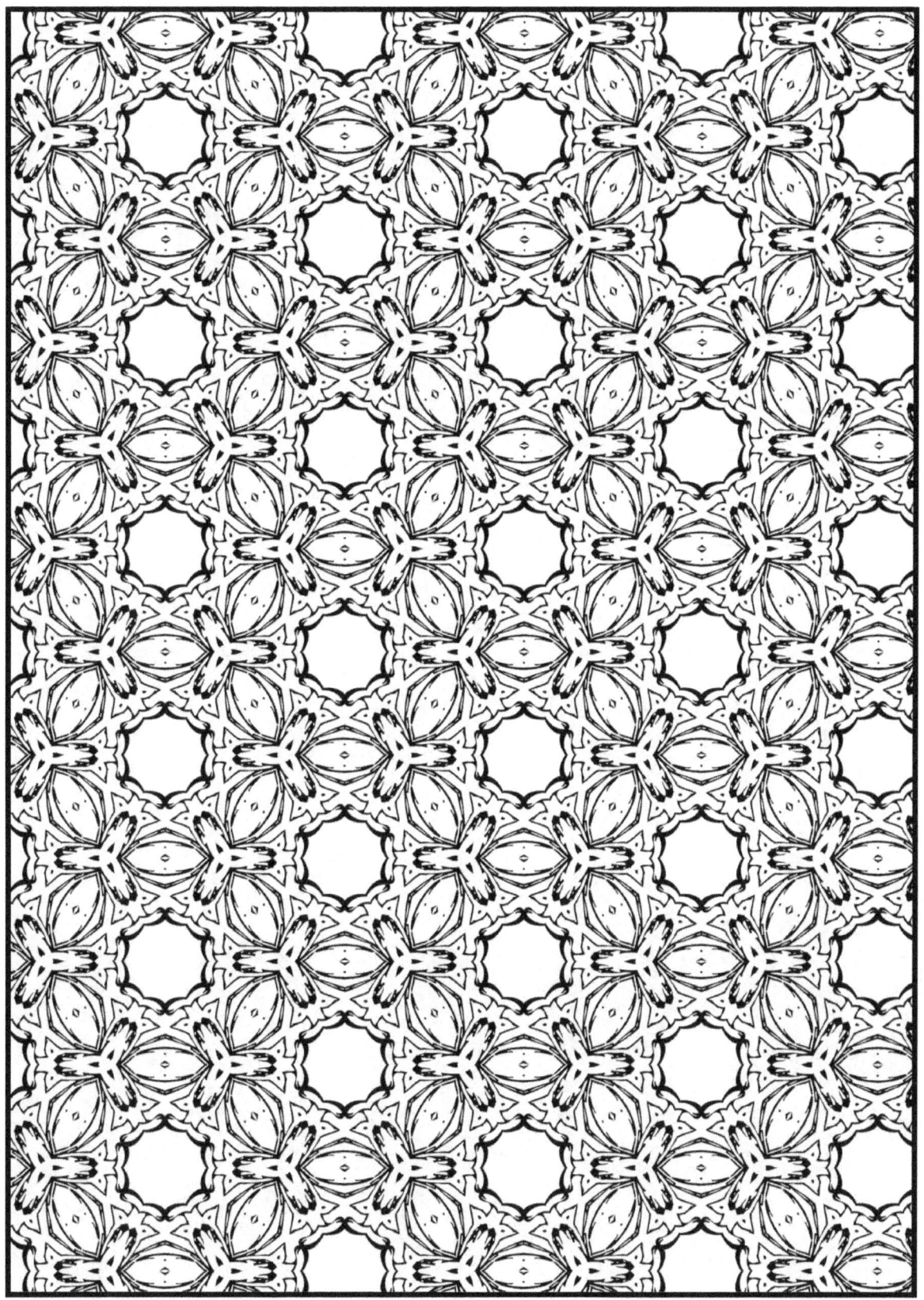

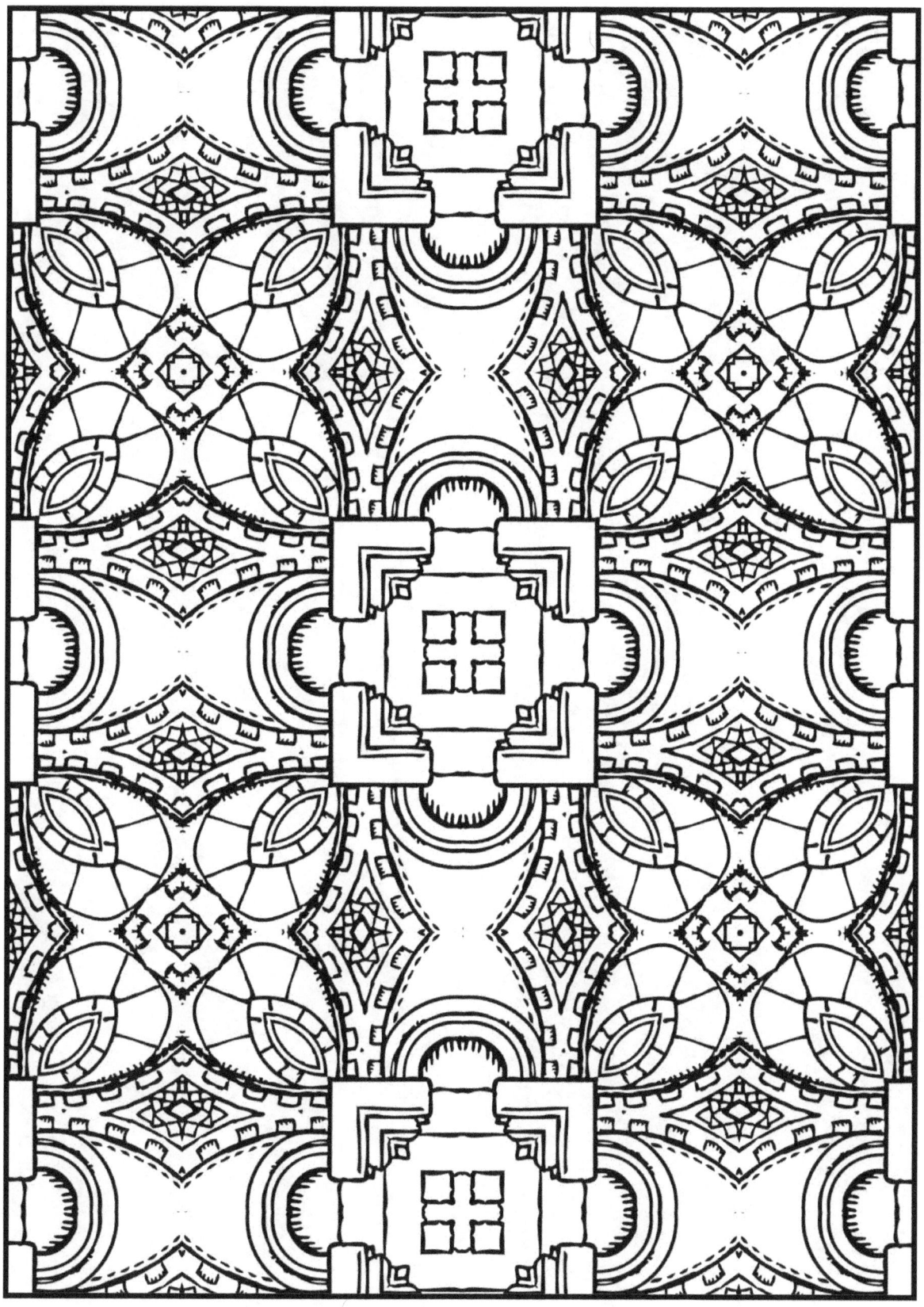

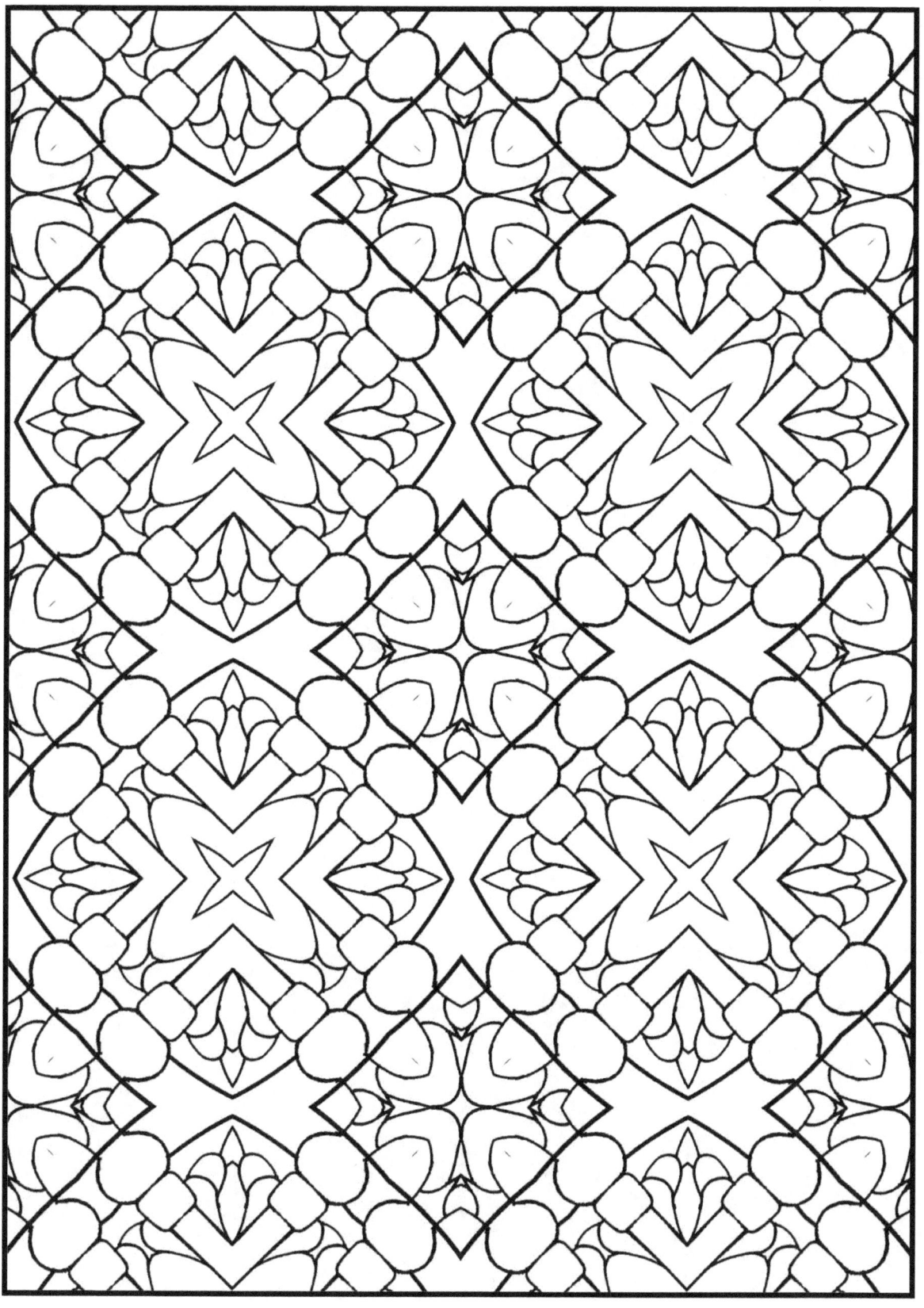

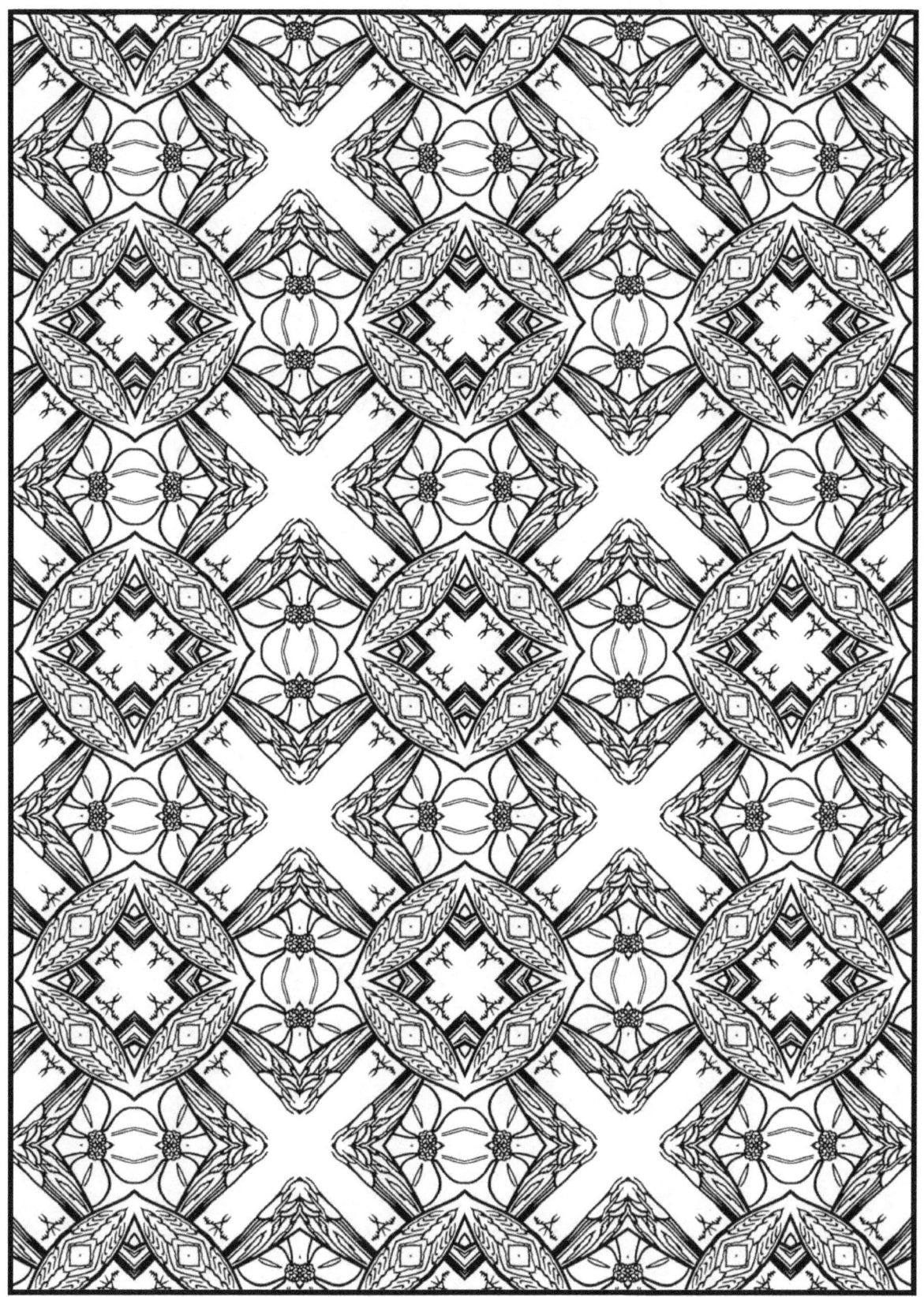

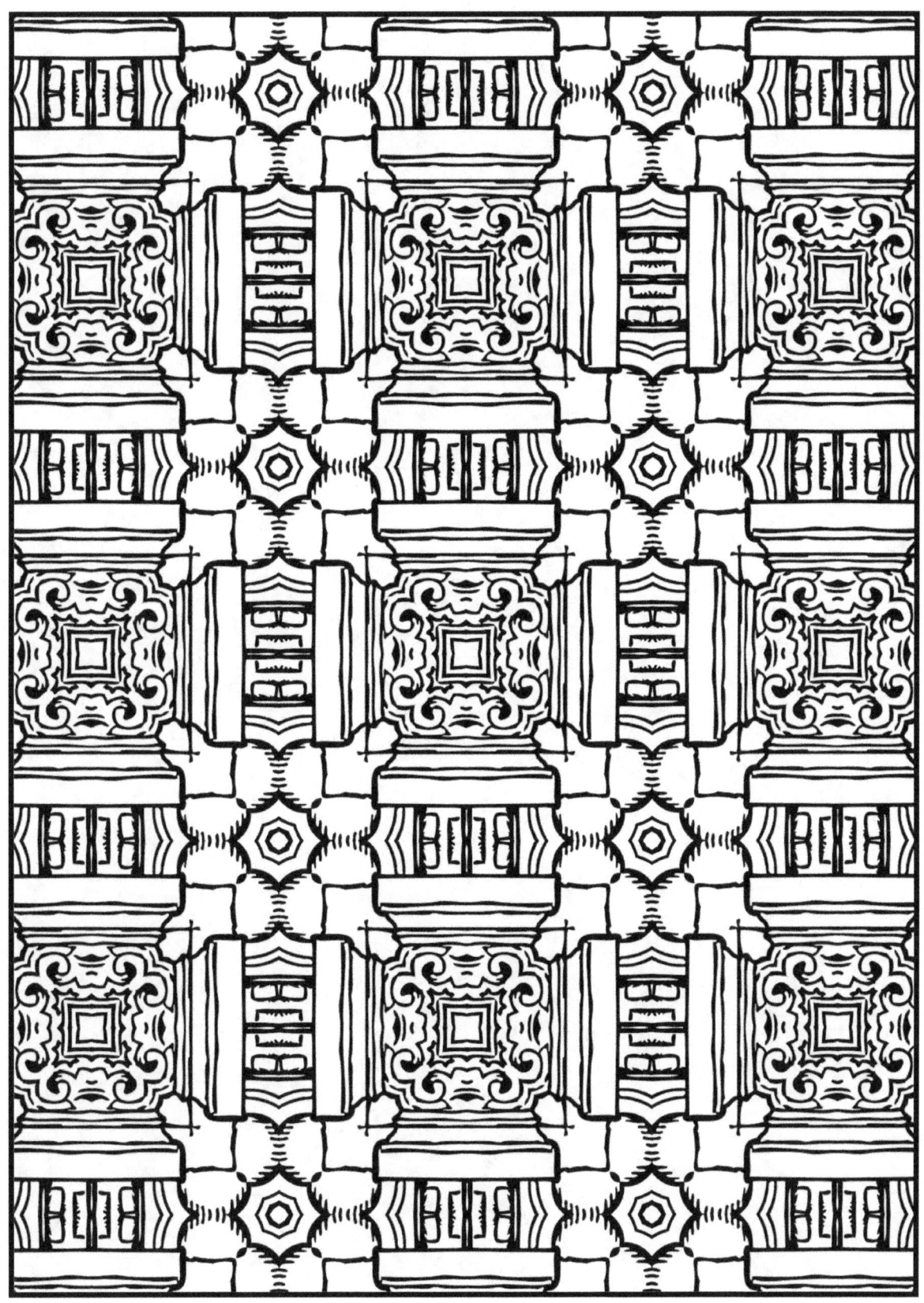

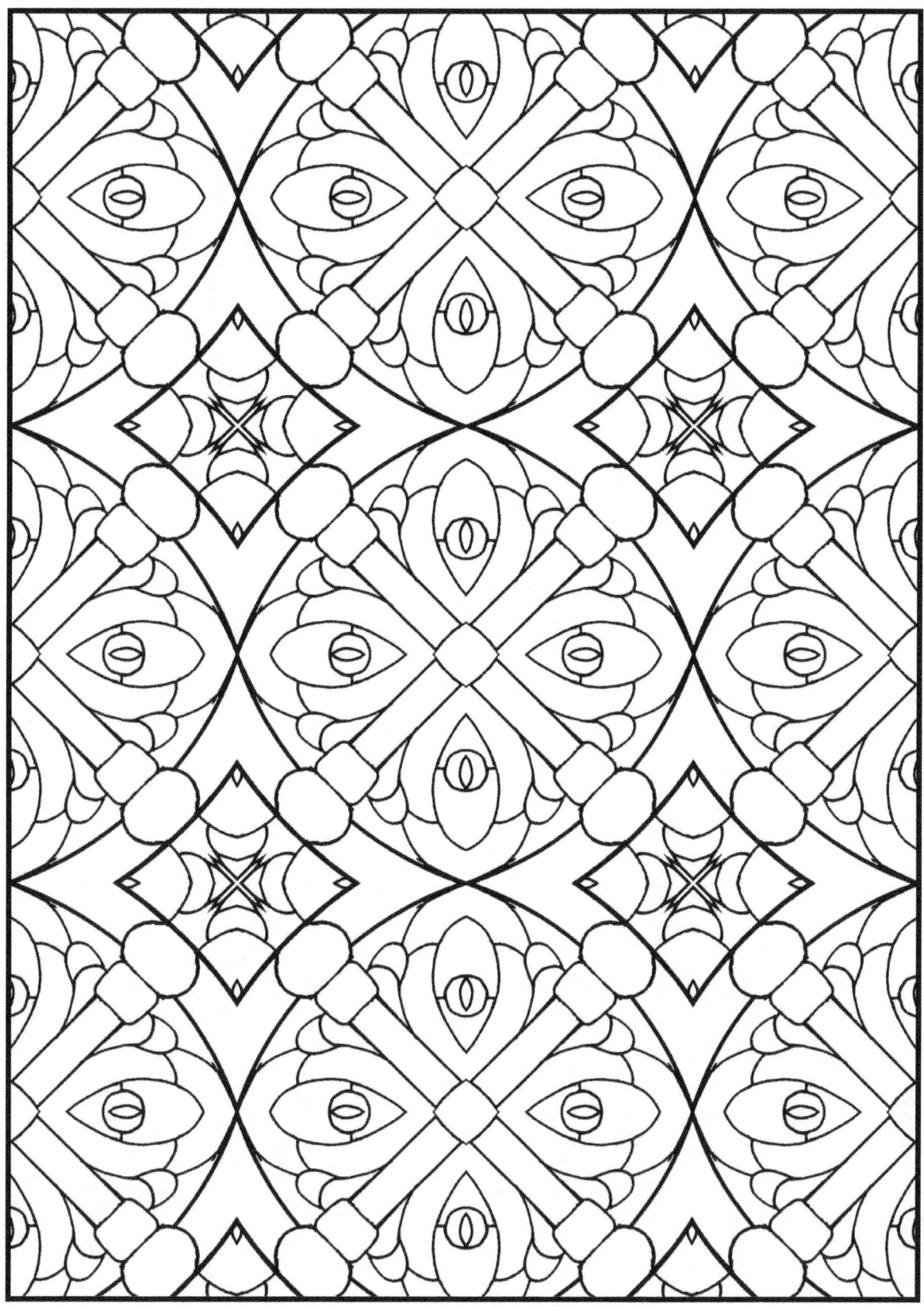

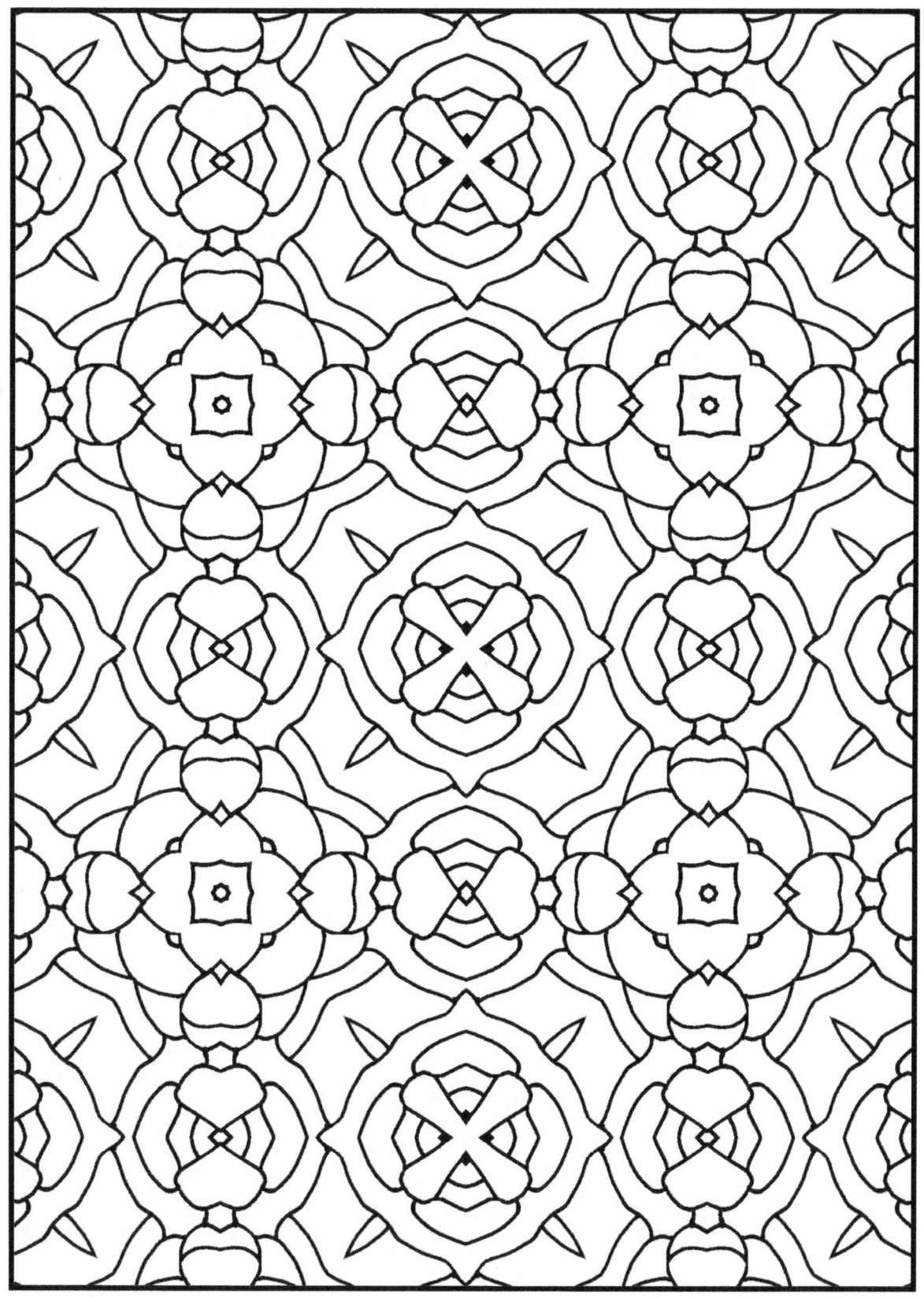

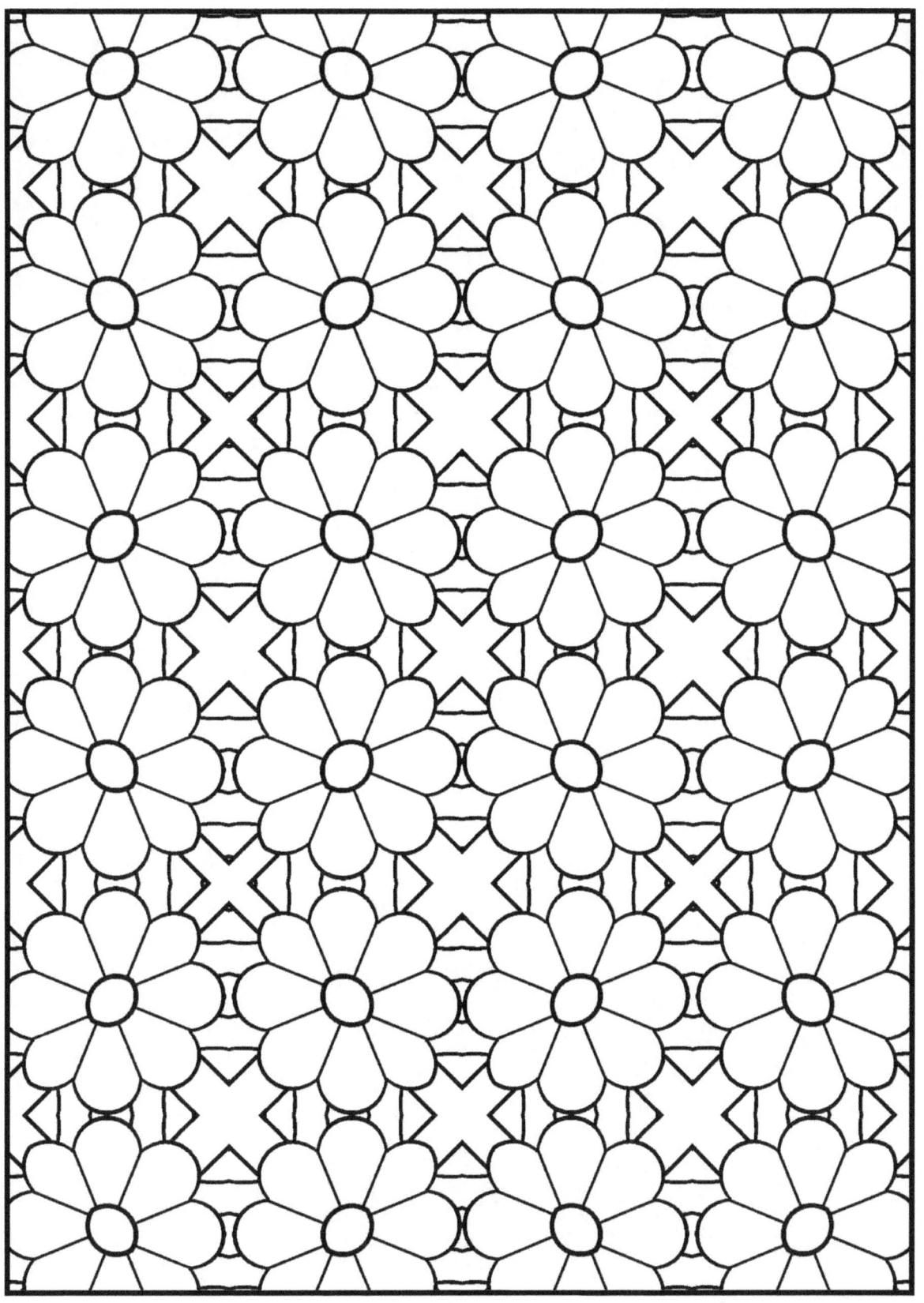

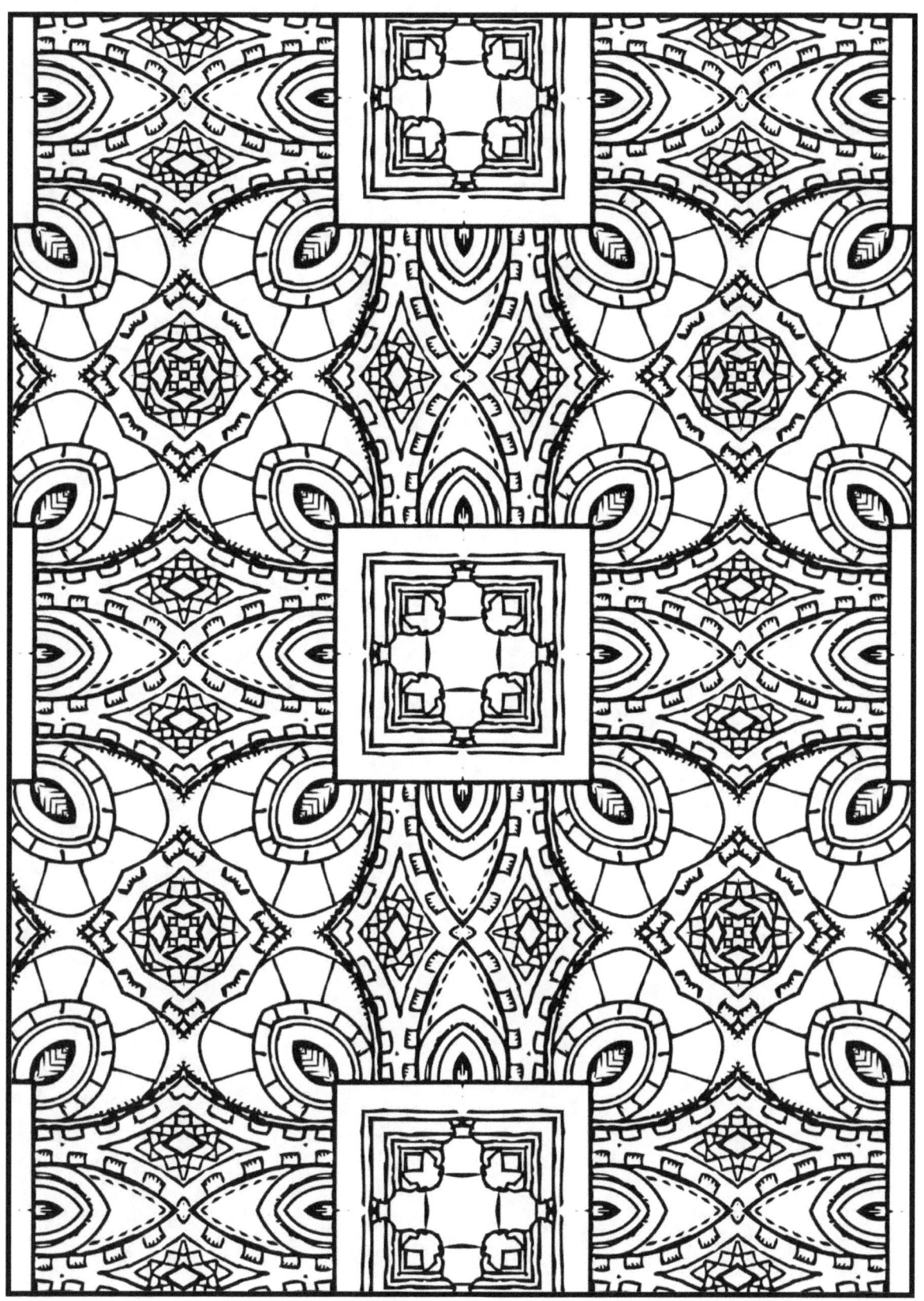

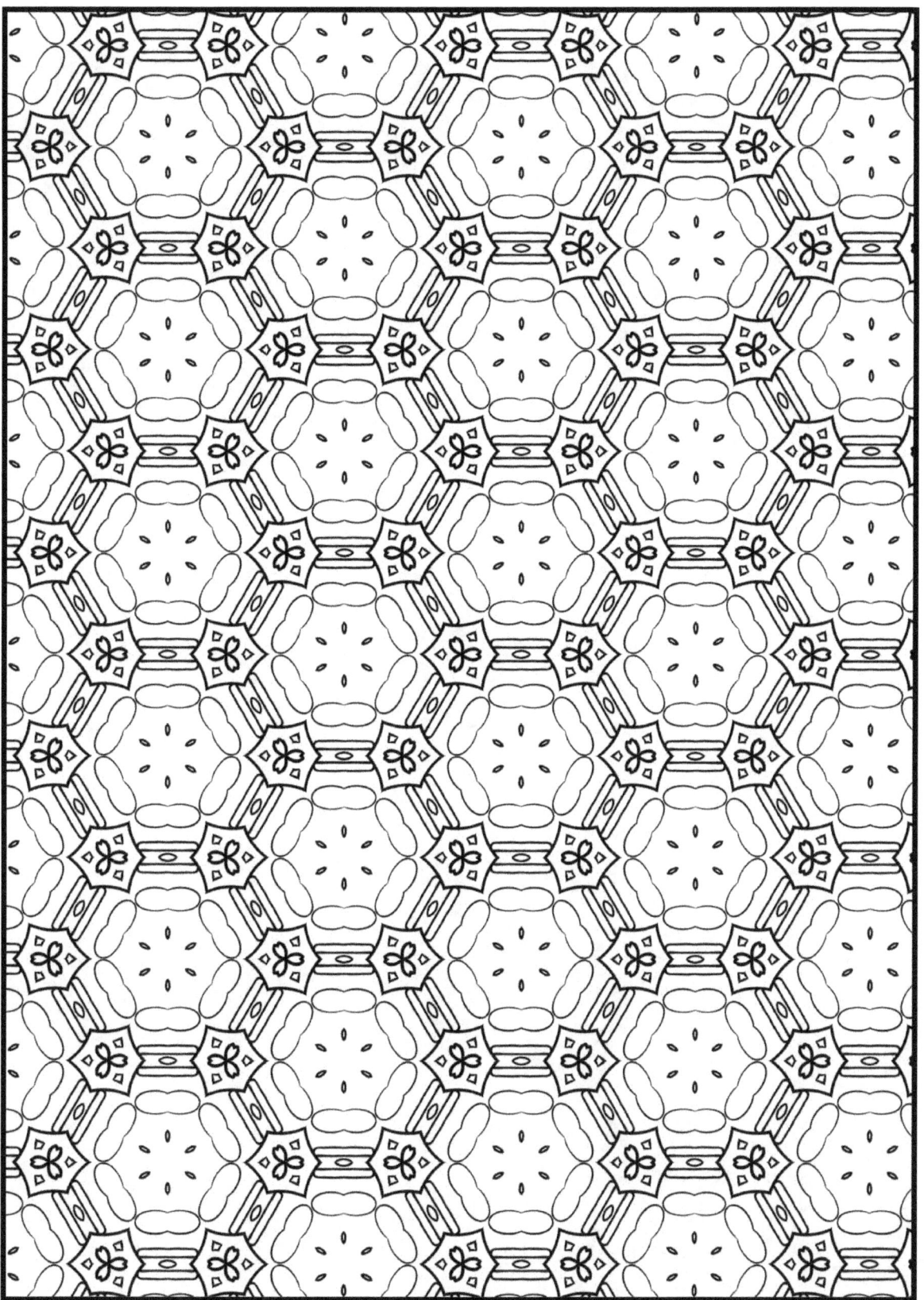

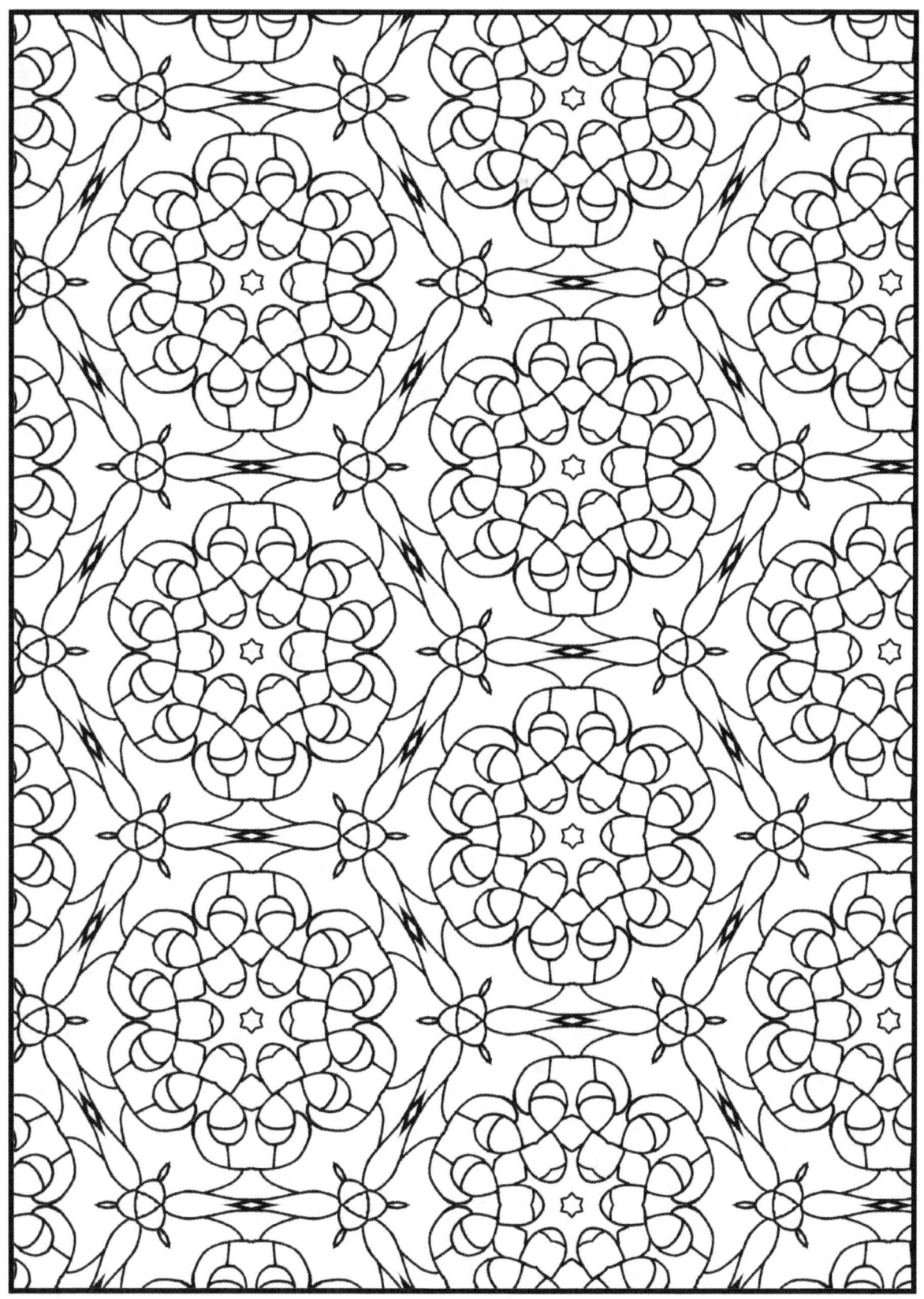

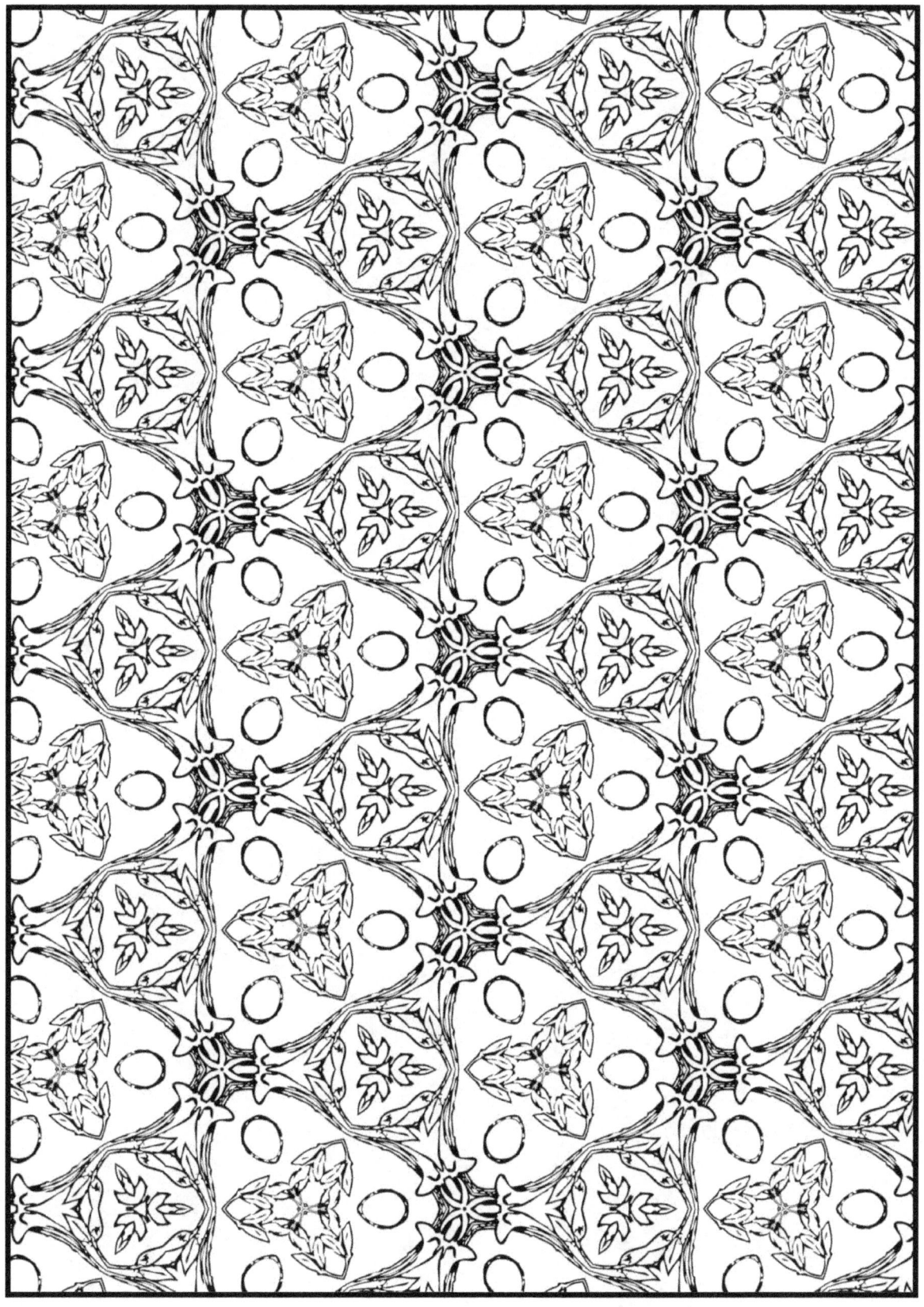

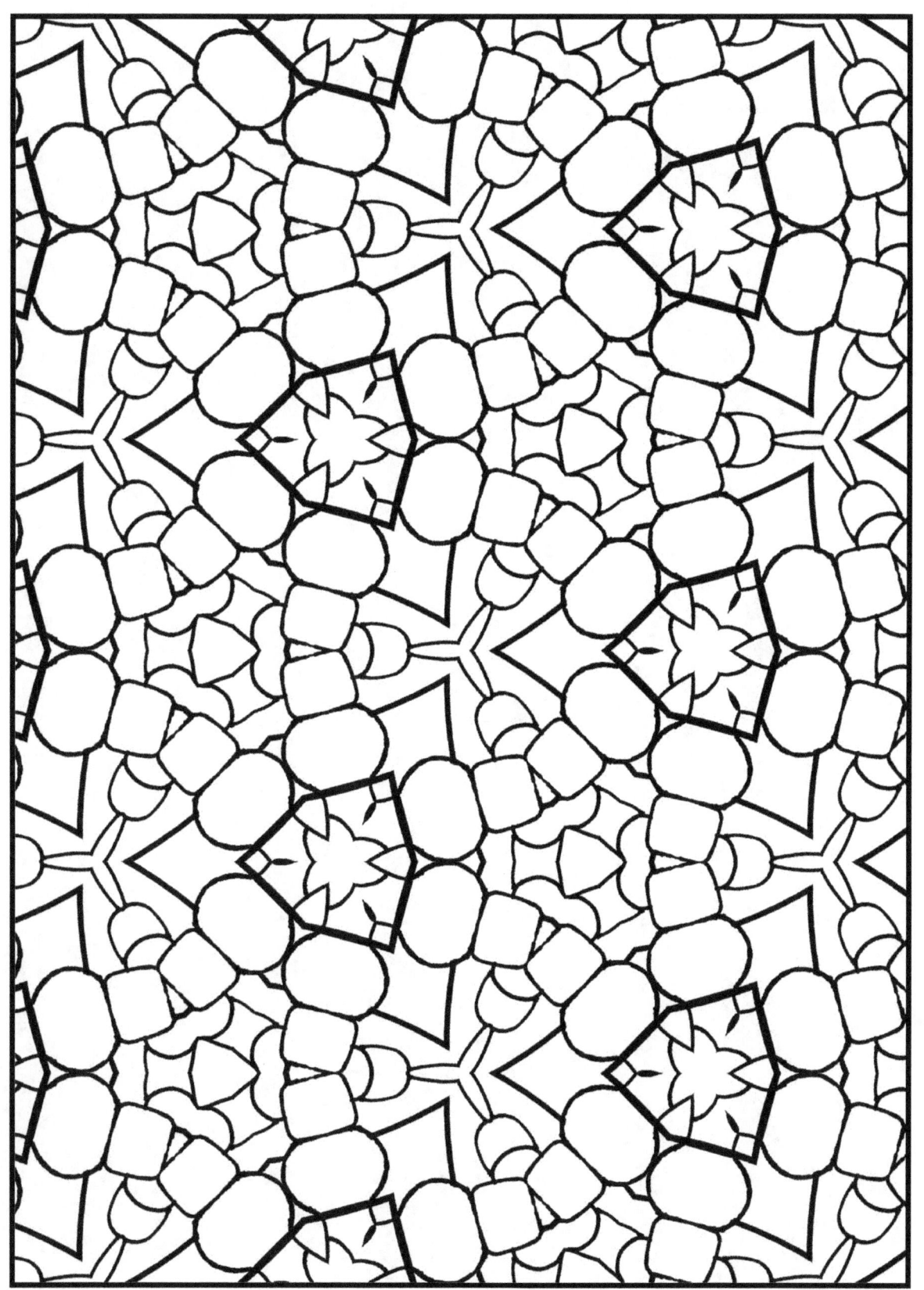

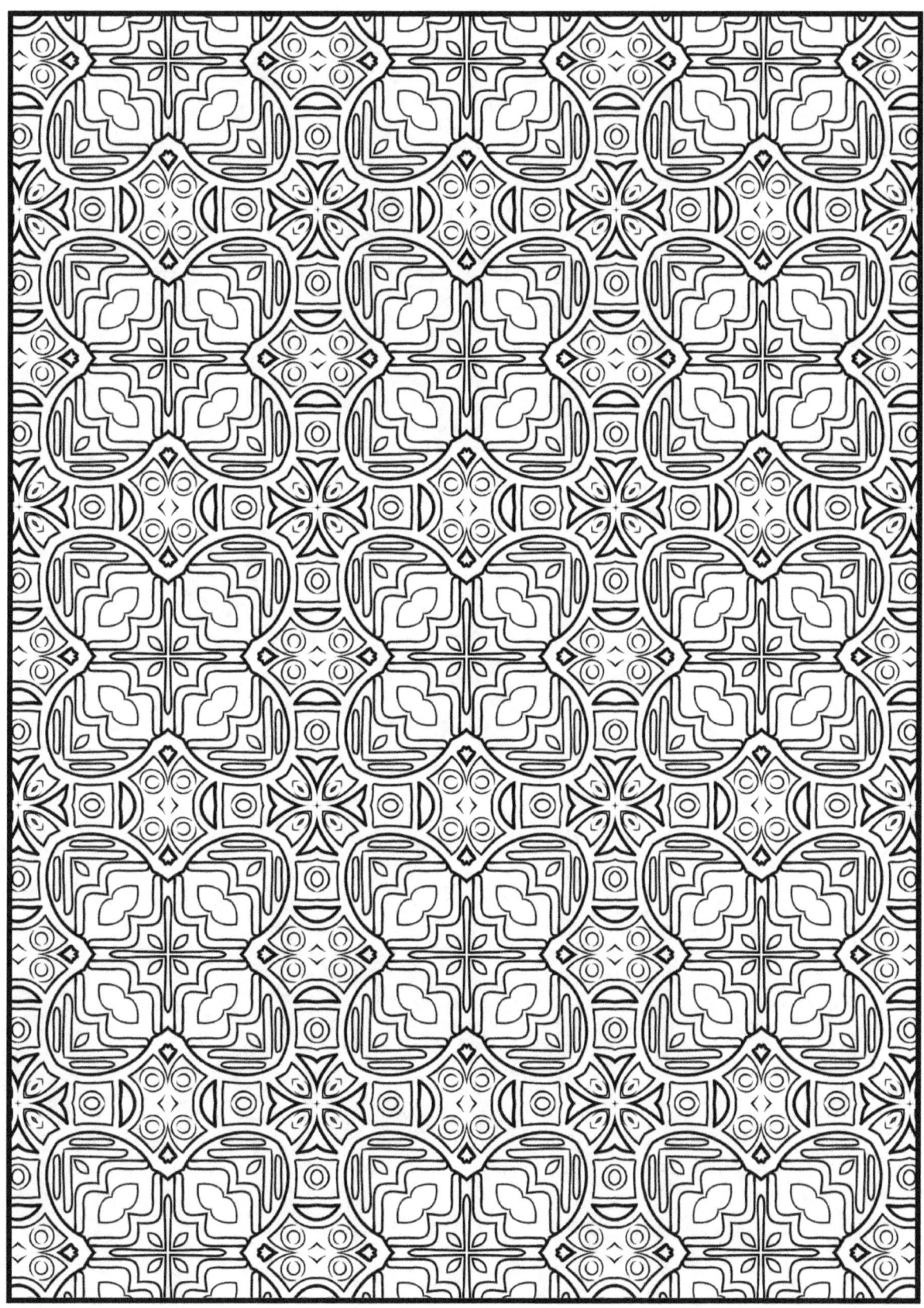

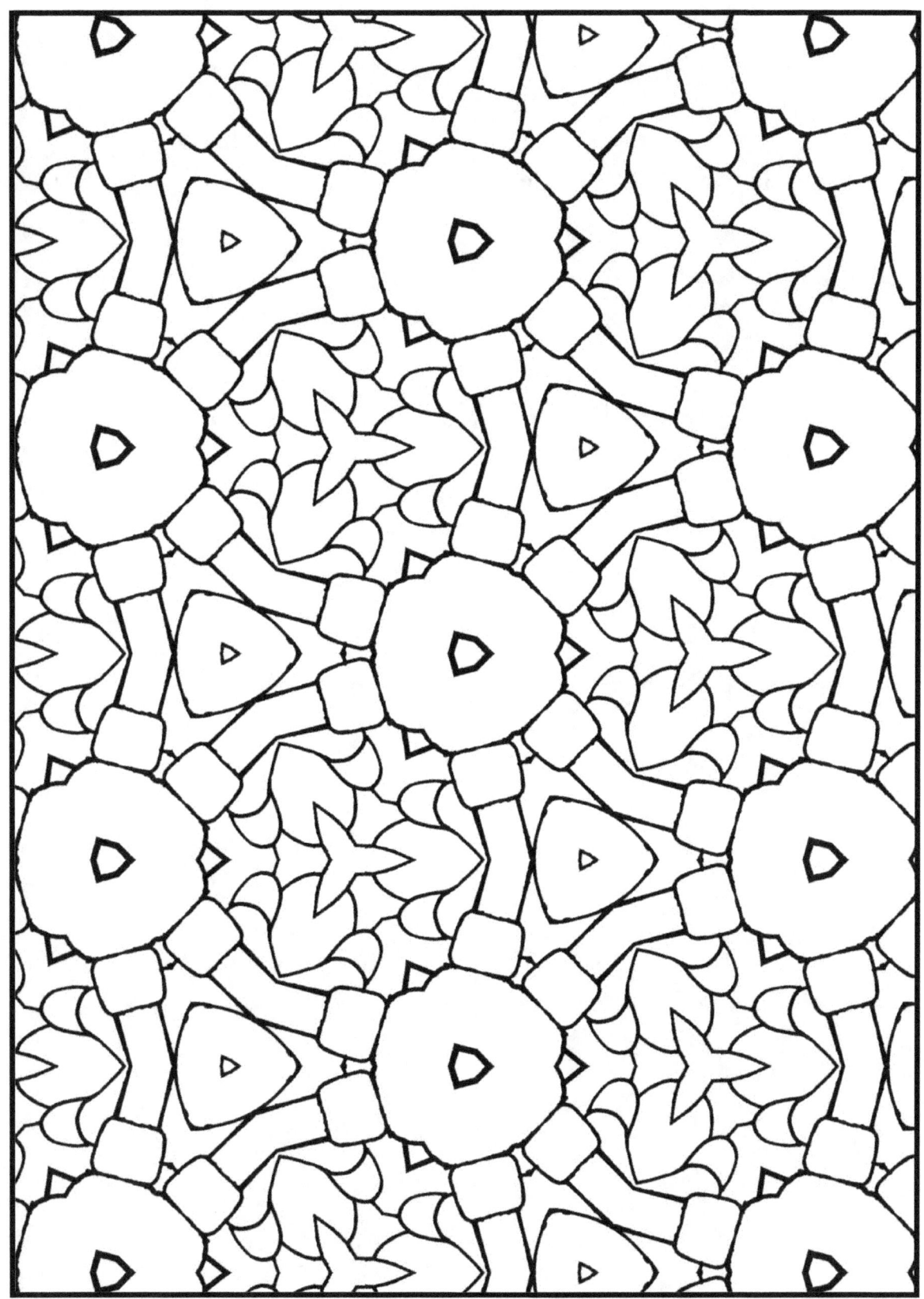

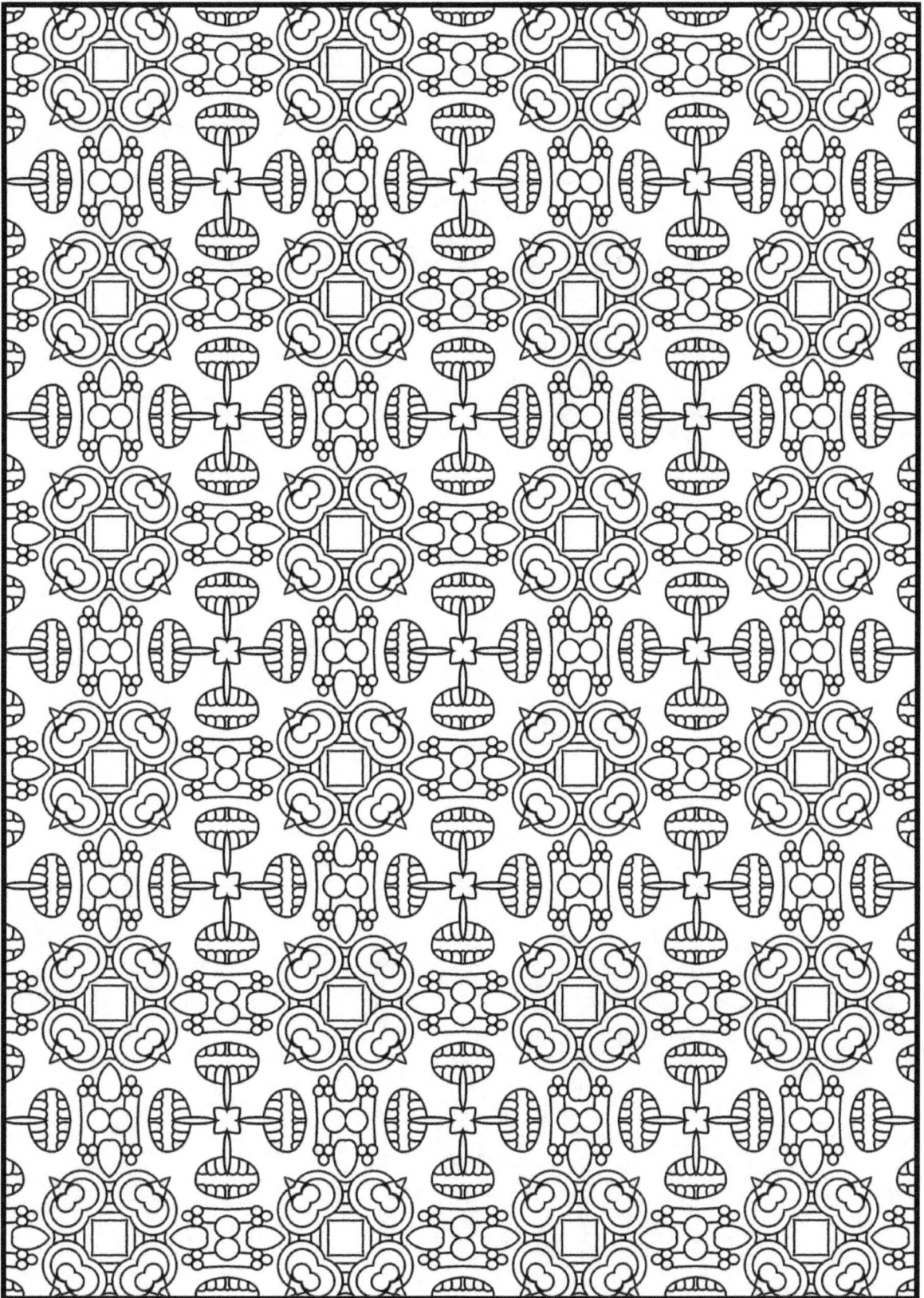

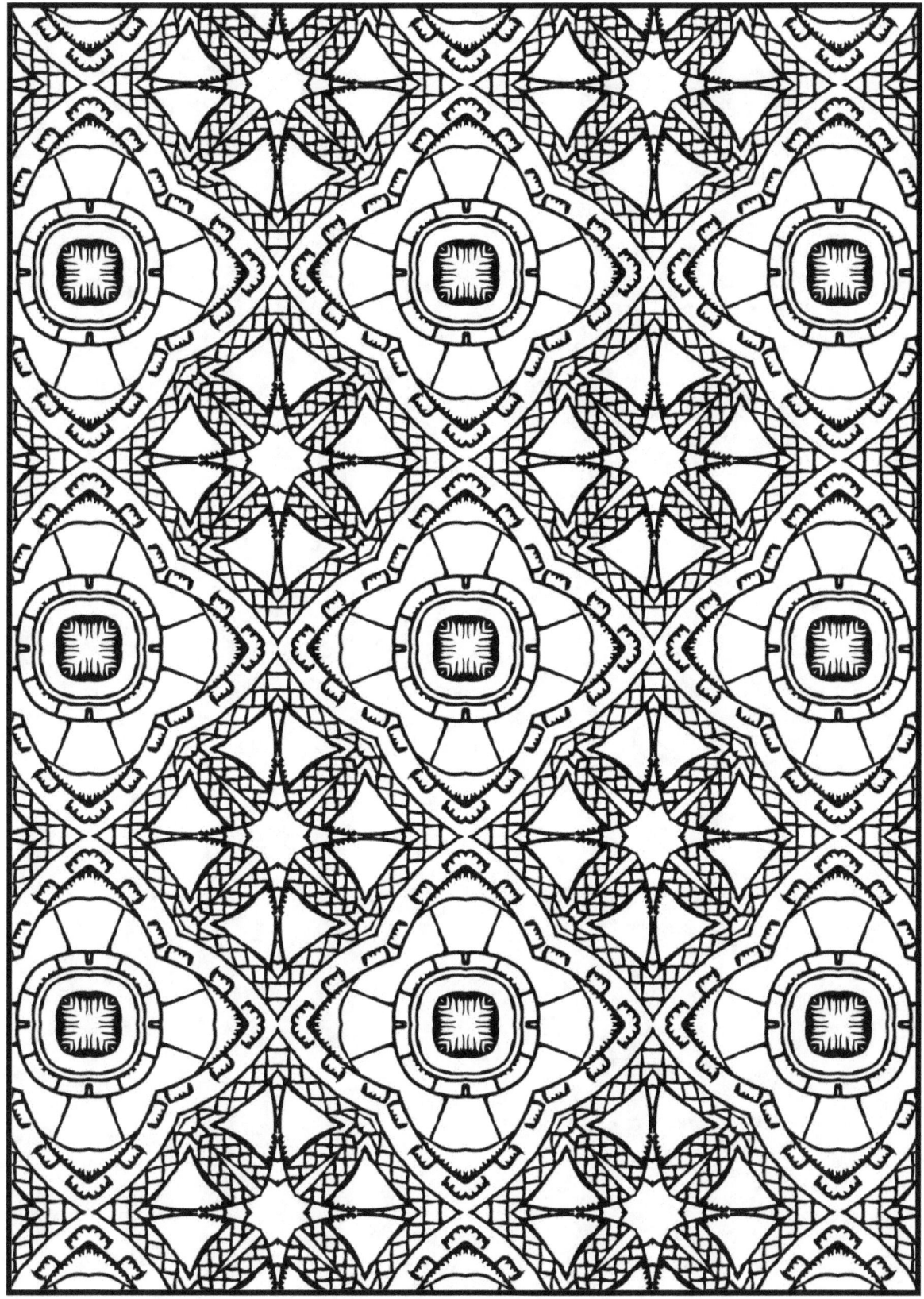

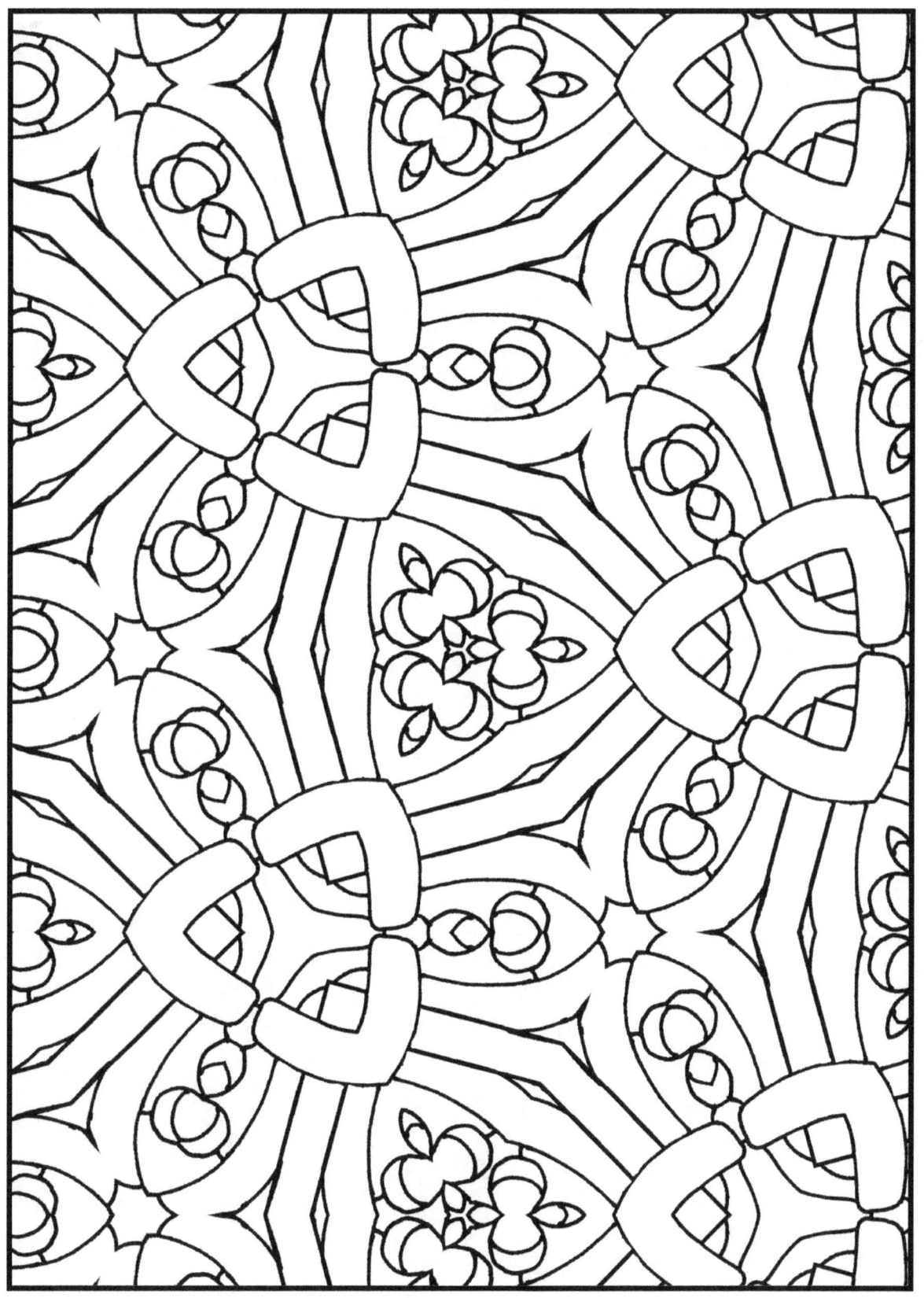

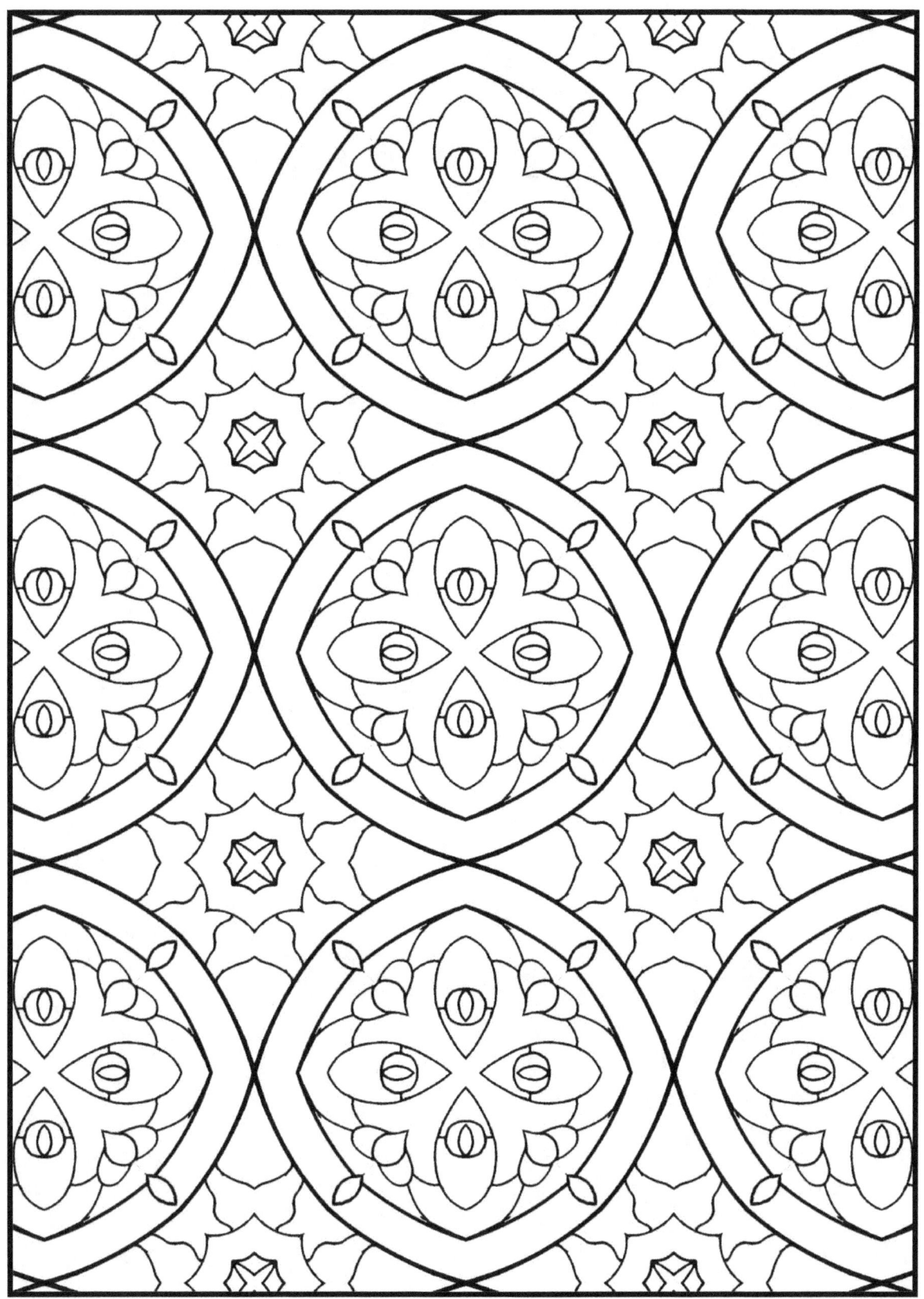

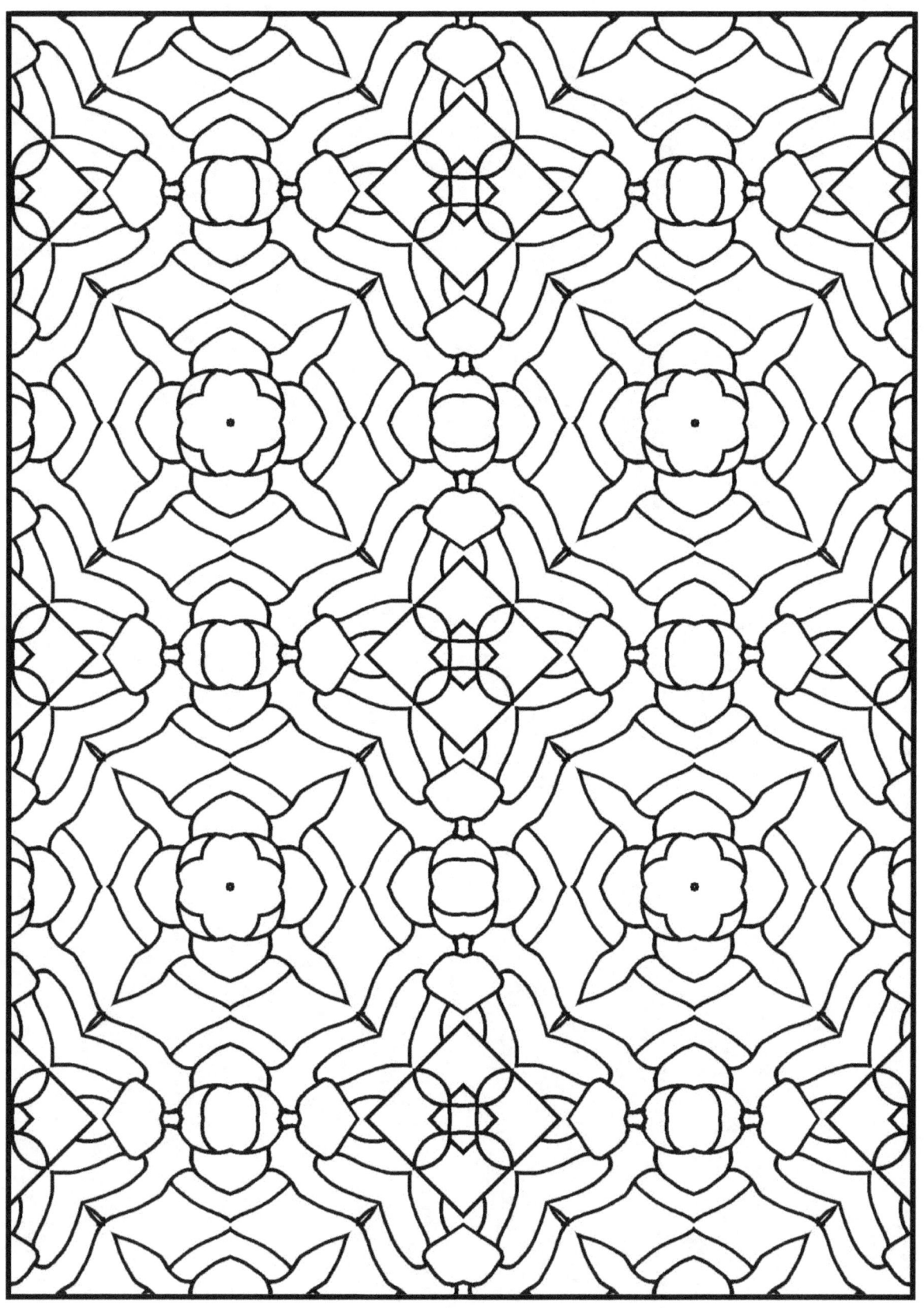

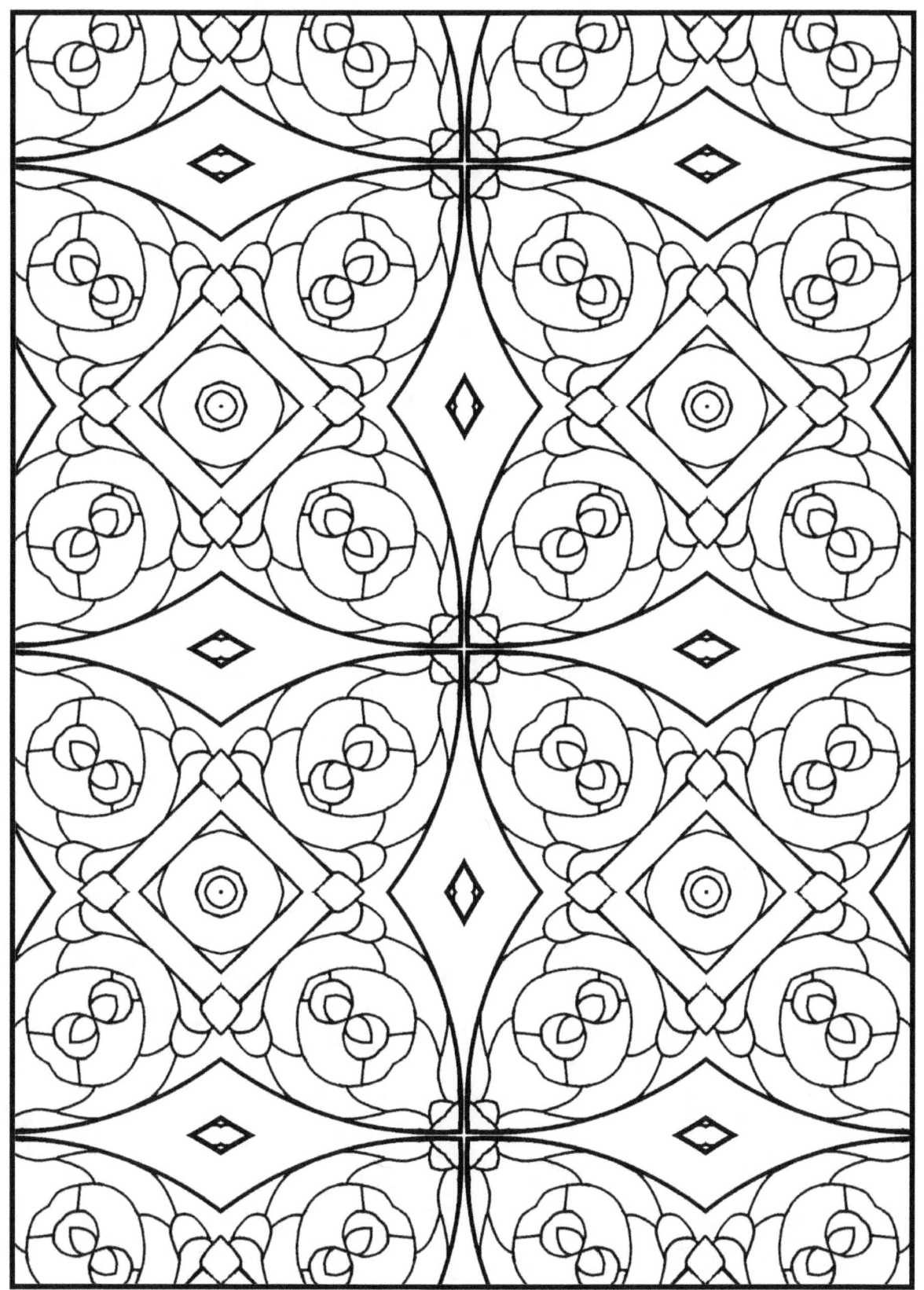

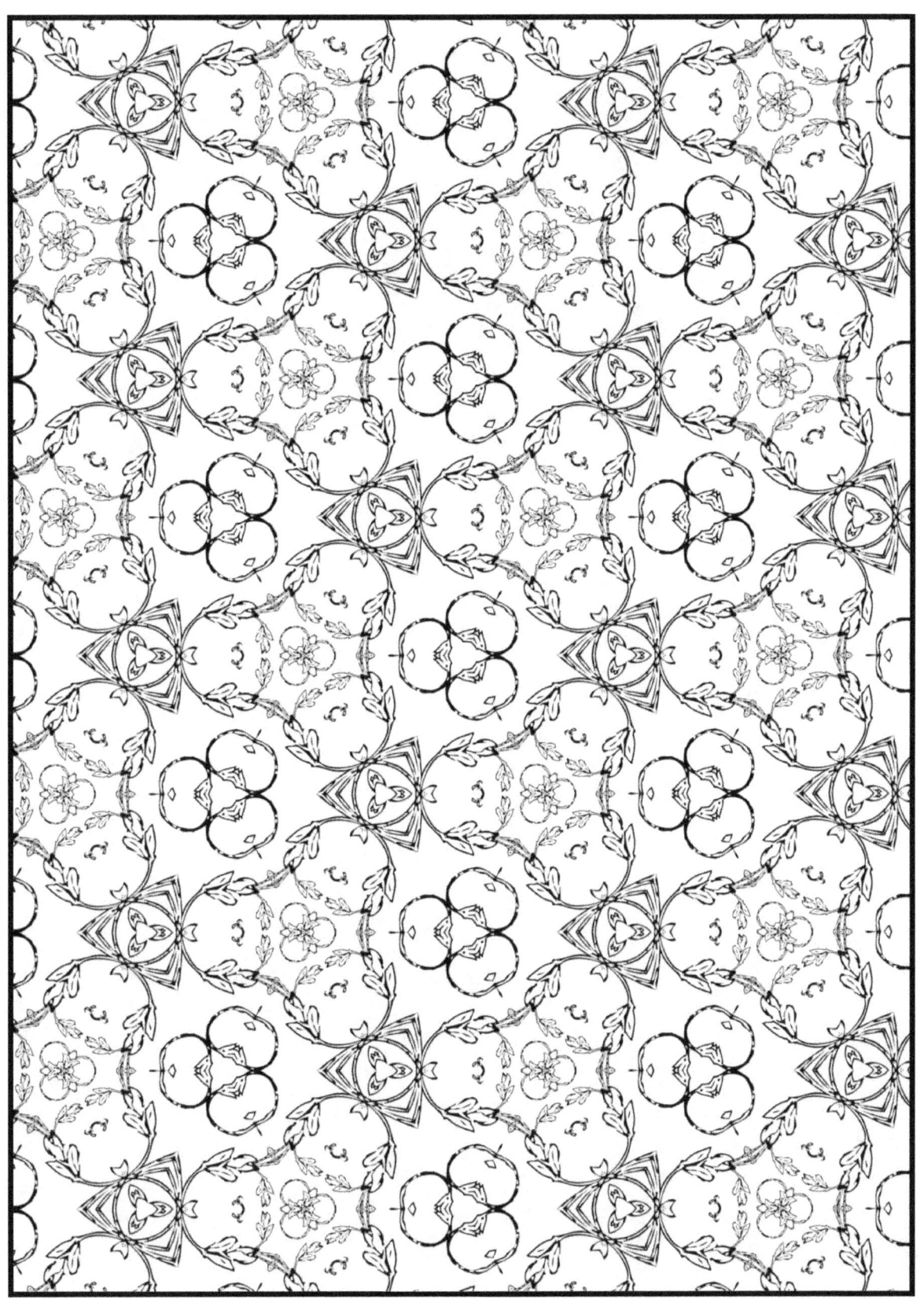

If you enjoyed the designs in this book, please visit our Facebook page to share your colorings and discover more designs, tips and fellow adult coloring fanatics:

www.facebook.com/adultcoloringbookscentral

www.ingramcontent.com/pod-product-compliance
Lightning Source LLC
Chambersburg PA
CBHW080552190526
45169CB00007B/2736